The Holdsworth Club

THE PROBLEMS OF A MASTER OF THE ROLLS

Being the Presidential Address of

THE RT. HON. SIR JOHN DONALDSON
MASTER OF THE ROLLS

PRESIDENT OF
THE HOLDSWORTH CLUB
of the Faculty of Law
in the University of Birmingham
1984—1985

Published by
The Holdsworth Club of the
University of Birmingham
1985

ISBN 07044 0774 4 ISSN 0307 0859

THE PROBLEMS OF A MASTER OF THE ROLLS

When I was asked to become President of the Holdsworth Club, my first reaction was one of delight. My second reaction was one of considerable trepidation, as it was borne in on me that such an honour could only be suitably acknowledged by an address which was worthy of it.

A necessary preliminary was to choose a subject. As others before me have found, this is far from easy for a variety of reasons, not least the expertise of the members of the Club and the wide range of topics covered in previous addresses.

I may say I was very tempted to update a lecture which I gave in Canada some years ago. My Canadian hosts chose the subject. It was "How to live with Her Majesty's Government, the employers' organisations and the trade unions without actually getting lynched". Topical though it would be, I reluctantly came to the conclusion that discretion must prevail.

Eventually inspiration, as I thought, came, in the middle of a visit to Japan last summer and I fixed on "The problems of a Master of the Rolls". As usual, the passage of time has made the choice seem rather less inspired, but I proffer it—both subject and problem—as a poor thing may be, but very definitely my own. The source of the inspiration was a visiting card with which I was bidden to equip myself for the visit. One side proclaimed in English that I was the Master of the Rolls. The other side, I sincerely hope, said much the same thing in Japanese. But it rapidly became clear that neither side conveyed the slightest hint of my professional occupation.

Now you may wonder why I should have expected the Japanese to know anything of the activities of a Master of the Rolls in the 1980's. Of course I did not, but the blank expression on the faces of my hosts brought back memories of similar expressions on the faces of our fellow countrymen, many of whom were lawyers. I do not blame them. I had been a judge for sixteen years, three of them spent as a member of the Court of Appeal, before I was appointed the 69th Master of the Rolls. It was only then that I began to discover what the office was all about.

One of my first surprises was to find that on appointment I ceased to be one of the "ordinary judges of the Court of Appeal". I seemed to be driven into outer darkness and was again required to take the oath of allegiance and the judicial oath, almost as if they had not "taken" on previous occasions. I then joined the Lord Chancellor, ex-Lord Chancellors, Lords of Appeal in Ordinary, the Lord Chief Justice, the President of the Family Division and the Vice-Chancellor as one of the *ex-officio* members of the Court. However, surprising though this may be, it is logically correct. I hold the same office as that held by John de Kirkby in 1265, probably the first Master of the Rolls. Over the centuries the office has had an unbroken existence. All that has changed has been the activitiesand duties of the holder of the office. And they are still changing.

The early Masters of the Rolls were royal archivists and it was only in 1958 that control of the Public Record Office passed from the Master of the Rolls to the Lord Chancellor. No doubt early Masters of the Rolls were also royal advisers and later they were to move into politics. As late as 1862 Lord Romilly was a member of the House of Commons. The longest holder of the office, Sir John Trevor, who was Master of the Rolls from 1685–1689 and from 1693–1717, was not only a member of the House of Commons. He was also the Speaker. He was deprived of the office of Speaker for corruptly accepting a bribe from the Corporation of London, but no one seems to have thought that this unfitted him to continue as Master of the Rolls which he did for many years thereafter. Whilst, on appointment, I knew that politics and corruption were no longer considered compatible with the office, no one had ever told me that links still existed with the office as it originally was.

Thus I found that I was, in theory at least, still responsible for the Chancery records and that I was Chairman of the Advisory Committee on Public Records. This is a body of experts which meets quarterly to monitor the work of government departments in selecting records for preservation for posterity and, equally important, calls for explanations when departments seek to restrict public access to those records. I understand that this link may not be maintained very much longer, because the view is taken, with which I personally agree, that there is no reason to expect a modern Master of the Rolls to have any of the necessary qualifications for membership of this Committee and certainly I do not.

Next, I found that, by section 133 of the Supreme Court Act, 1981, I was the authority charged with the duty of regulating the enrolment or filing of instruments in the Supreme Court. In practical terms this only creates problems in relation to changes of name by deed poll. I had vaguely known that there was such a procedure, but I was brought up in an era when the most effective way to change your name was to apply to the Food and National Registration offices to have your ration and identity cards amended and I knew that countless unmarried couples adopted the same surname without further formality. To my surprise I found that I was responsible for making regulations governing the circumstances in which such deeds could be officially registered and indeed had to make new rules last year to take account of the British Nationality Act, 1981.

There are about 300 such deeds registered each year, but happily the day to day administration is the responsibility of the Senior Queen's Bench Master and his staff. I become involved only if he refuses to register a deed and the applicant asks that the matter be referred to me personally. Such refusals can occur where one spouse reasonably refuses to concur in a change sought by the other or where a minor is involved and the change is not in his best interests.

One reference to me, following a refusal by the Senior Master, raised a not uninteresting problem. I had personal knowledge of the family concerned and, on ordinary judicial principles, would have disqualified myself and asked another judge to act. But I found that the jurisdiction was that of the Master of the Rolls as such and could not be delegated, so I had to reach a decision. Happily I was able to suggest an amendment in the deed which met the Senior Master's very proper objectives and was acceptable to the applicant.

Another of the duties which reflects the office as it used to be is my responsibility in relation to manorial documents under section 144A of the Law of Property Act, 1922. My concern is that they shall be retained in proper custody and be properly preserved. Again I am relieved of the routine administrative duties involved. These are undertaken by the Secretary of the Royal Commision on Historical Manuscripts, but from time difficulties arise which have to be discussed, considered and resolved in one way or another.

More recent accretions to the duties of the office have been that of Visitor to University College, London and to Nuffield College, Oxford. Neither office has proved in the least onerous and I welcome the connection with academic life.

This brings me to the largest and most important Roll with which I am concerned—the Roll of Solicitors. Happily it is kept by The Law Society on a computer, but every month I have to authorise the addition of the names of those who have just qualified and each year over 4,000 new solicitors are presented with specimens of my illegible signature on their admission certificates. I confess that at times I have been tempted to invest in a machine which would reproduce my signature mechanically, but have been deterred by the reflection that if the solicitor has devoted 5 years to qualifying, it was churlish to begrudge the few seconds necessary to sign the admission certificate which I hope will be framed and hung in not too inappropriate a place. Admission ceremonies take place about 15 times a year and usually it is the President of The Law Society who presents the certificates, but once a year it is my privilege to do so myself.

Alas there is a less pleasant aspect of my connection with the Roll of Solicitors. In a profession which consists of 50,000 practising members, it is inevitable that some will behave in a manner which is inconsistent with their continued membership. The decision to strike them off the Roll of Solicitors or to authorise their restoration is a matter for the independent Disciplinary Tribunal. However I have to appoint the members of that Tribunal, which includes lay members, and whereas an appeal against an order striking off lies to the High Court, appeals against a refusal to restore to the Roll are heard by me as Master of the Rolls.

It is also my duty to hear appeals from decisions by the Tribunal refusing to revoke orders forbidding the employment of particular individuals as clerks to solicitors without the consent of The Law Society. In addition, I hear appeals from solicitors who are aggrieved at decisions by the Council for the Law Society to refuse a practising certificate or to attach conditions to it.

These are depressing jurisdictions to exercise, because so often the appellant has made considerable efforts to rehabilitate himself and has done so in very difficult circumstances. Furthermore his legal skill is usually his principal asset. However I have to remind myself that I am not concerned simply with the situation of the individual appellant. I have to have regard to the need to maintain public confidence in a profession upon whose probity and responsibility the whole system for administering justice depends. Traditionally both branches of the profession are stern and, by some standards, unforgiving taskmasters. But, for the reasons which I have given, it should and must be so.

I am glad to say that my connection with the solicitors' profession is by no means confined to admissions and disciplinary matters. The Council of the Law Society has very wide statutory powers entitling it to make regulations governing many aspects of professional practice and these regulations need my formal concurrence. This produces something in the nature of a statutory partnership. The senior partner is rightly the Council of the Law Society, whose members have vast experience of the needs and problems of the profession. However I like to think that I can make a contribution and I have been very fortunate in the extent to which the Council has taken me into its confidence. Thus we have had extensive discussions on such matters as advertising and the selling of houses by solicitors as part of their professional activities. As is well known in the profession, I refused to concur in certain regulations governing professional insurance, largely upon the grounds that they were, in my view, *ultra vires*. This was a wholly exceptional situation and one which I do not expect to occur again in the light of the very close relationship which has now been established.

However I should not like it to be thought that I am solely dependent upon "the establishment" for information about the solicitors' profession. It is my pleasure to attend various social gatherings of local law societies and this gives me an opportunity to talk to individual members. Furthermore members of the public have little hesitation in writing to me about every aspect of the law and its administration and inevitably this includes complaints about solicitors and about the administration of legal aid which is another Law Society responsibility. Where there is anything which requires investigation, I consult the Law Society and I should make it clear that I have been most impressed by the service which I have received. I have also come to sympathise with the task of those Law Society officials who have to deal with complaints from the public. The art of putting forward facts in a coherent form and refraining from abusing not only the person who is the subject of the complaint, but also the person to whom the complaint is addressed, appears to be in the very early stages of development.

Thus far I have said nothing about the duties, and problems, of the Master of the Rolls in relation to the Court of Appeal, save the notice, in passing, that he is one of several *ex officio* members. It is a curious feature of the Supreme Court Act, 1981, that whereas it provides that the Lord Chief Justice is President of the Queen's Bench Division, the Vice-Chancellor the President of the Chancery Division and the President of the Family Division President of that Division, there is no President of the Court of Appeal. Instead the Court is divided into a Criminal Division, whose President is the Lord Chief Justice, and a Civil Division, whose President is the Master of the Rolls. Even more curious is the power, which has never been exercised, to appoint a single Vice-President for both divisions.

In practice, in so far as there is any need for a President of the Court of Appeal as a whole, that need is met by the Master of the Rolls.

I say "in so far as there is any need" because the need is very limited. Indeed I can only think of three areas in which it arises.

The first is in relation to the allocation of members of the Court as between the Civil and Criminal Divisions. Clearly this is as much the concern of the Lord Chief Justice as of the Master of the Rolls and they must and do consult each other. However, someone has to take the initiative and it is the Master of the Rolls who does so in nominating an appropriate number of Lords Justices to sit in the Criminal Division for what are usually three week tours of duty. At present that number is four out of a total strength of 21. If the relatively small number of Lord Justices sitting in the Criminal Division is thought to be surprising, it must be remembered that the usual constitution of a Court in that Division is the Lord Chief Justice or a Lord Justice sitting with one or two puisne Judges. In recent times it has become customary for one of the Queen's Bench Divisional Courts also to have a Lord Justice as the Presiding Judge, but this need is met from the allocation to the Criminal Division.

The second such area is in relation to maintaining the strength of the Court of Appeals as a whole. When numbers are depleted due to sickness or when, for any other reason, there is a need to increase its strength on a temporary basis, it is for the Master of the Rolls to ask the Lord Chancellor to exercise his power to invite a retired Lord Justice to return to duty in order to fill the gap.

The third is in relation to ascerting the collective view of the Court of Appeal, if it is sought, in relation to the reform of civil law and procedure, suitability of individuals for appointments and matters of that sort. Someone must make the necessary enquiries and collate the results and that someone is the Master of the Rolls. In relation to reform of the criminal law, any initiative would come from the Lord Chief Justice since the Master of the Rolls never concerns himself with that side of the law.

So I come to my principal activity, namely, as President of the Civil Division of the Court of Appeal. It is an office whose holder is, I hope, not without influence. But it is certainly an office without power and that is as it should be.

We live in an age when "accountablity" is a concept much in vogue. When I was a puisne judge, I was twice asked to whom I was accountable. On one occasion my questioner was a Cabinet Minister. On the other a member of the House of Lords with vast experience of government. Both were astonished and, I think, somewhat dismayed, when I replied "To no-one other than myself". Yet they should have been delighted. It is generally accepted that the independence of the judiciary is one of the cornerstones of our liberties. But that independence must be not only a collective, but also an individual independence.

I mention this matter lest anyone should be so misguided as to think that there was any relationship of accountability between the Master of the Rolls and the Lords Justices. Nothing could be further from the truth. A somewhat pompous description of my position would "*primus inter pares*"—a description sometimes applied to the Prime Minister in relation to the Cabinet. Whilst there is no comparison between the nature and importance of the two offices, there are parallels. The Cabinet and the Court of Appeal are of similar size and must be amongst the largest bodies composed exclusively of Privy Councillors. I have also heard it suggested, *sotto voce*, that both are composed exclusively of *prima donnas*. But there are two vital differences. First the Court of Appeal does not accept collective responsibility for judicial decisions. Second, unlike the Prime Minister, the Master of the Rolls can neither hire nor fire.

I think that a more accurate description of my role would be "choirmaster". I do my best to encourage harmony, but have no power to enforce it. Furthermore, whilst I do indeed sing in Court 3 as a member of the choir, I do not personally regard it as any part of my function as Master of the Rolls to seek to be a soloist, a role for which I do not regard myself as particularly well suited.

I was appointed at a time when the work of the Court and the Court itself had experienced considerable expansion. At the turn of the century there were five Lord Justices and it was not until the Second World War that this was increased to eight. When, in 1962, Lord Denning was appointed as Master of the Rolls in succession to Lord Evershed, there were still only 11. Now there are 21—as large a team as the Queen's Bench Division in 1950 when Lord Goddard was Chief Justice. Clearly the administrative system which was appropriate to a much smaller court needed drastic revision and it was my good fortune to succeed to the office at the time when some of those changes, already recommended by a Committee under the Chairmanship of Lord Scarman, were about to be put into effect.

This is not the time or the place for a detailed exposition of the old and the new systems. In any event the information is readily available elsewhere. Suffice it to say that in Lord Denning's time, there was no Civil Appeals Office as such, no Registrar of Civil Appeals and there was no power enabling a single Lord Justice to deal with incidental applications. Furthermore the power enabling two Lords Justices to constitute a Court of Appeal was more limited than it is today. The administration of the Court was wholly in the hands of the Master of the Rolls and his clerk, the senior Lord Justices, who normally preside, and their clerks, assisted by the clerks to the other Lords Justices. And all judicial decisions had to be taken by a court consisting of at least 2, and usually 3, Lords Justices.

The advent of the new system has enabled me to decentralise much of the day-to-day decision-making. Thus it is the Registrar who prepares the constitution lists determining who sits with whom and for how long and which appeals are heard by which court. This is not to say that I am not involved. I take a close interest in evolving the principles which are to be applied and when, as frequently occurs, special situations arise in which it is necessary to make adjustments, I expect to be and am consulted. I am also concerned with such questions as the extent to which we should use the power to hear appeals before two judge courts. So let me say a word about the principles which I apply.

Any change in the constitution of a court is wasteful of court time, since, as the time for a change in constitution approaches, it becomes increasingly difficult to fit in a long appeal. The ideal, from this point of view, would be to have the same Lords Justices sitting together in perpetuity. This would, however, drive them mad and would deprive us of the benefit of the cross-pollination of ideas and approaches which is achieved by sitting with as many different Lords Justices as possible. Experience shows that a workable compromise is achieved if, in general, the constitution of the civil courts is changed about every six weeks and that of the criminal courts every three weeks.

The next problem concerns who sits with whom. This indirectly affects the allocation of appeal—who hears what. It would be possible to constitute courts consisting of those with the same specialist experience and to allocate that type of appeal to that court. In terms of saving time, this would be efficient, because a specialist judge can usually dispose of a matter much more quickly than can a judge to whom the topic is strange. Such a policy would, however, be open to three objections. First, and I speak as one who may be regarded as having once been a specialist, it is no bad thing to expose specialists to the influence of other minds which are unaffected by the accepted shibboleths. Second, it would be difficult to operate such a system and make substantial changes in the constitution of the court. The same judges would be sitting together most of the time. Third, listing and the estimation of the duration of appeals is an inexact science, if it is a science at all. Some appeals will overrun and some underrun their estimates. If appeals are to be processed smoothly, there will be a continual need to switch them from one court to another as unexpected gaps and congestions occur. This is much more difficult if you have specialised courts. Accordingly we have adopted the policy that there should be what might be described as multi-disciplinary courts, but that, where possible, no appeal on a specialist topic should be listed before a court, none of whose members are familiar with that speciality.

Whether an appeal should be listed before a two judge, as contrasted with the three judge, court depends, as a matter of jurisdiction, upon whether it is an interlocutory appeal or an appeal from the county court. The theoretical objection to a two judge court that it is a recipe for disagreement and is likely to involve the parties in the additional expense of a re-hearing is not borne out in practice. I therefore use this power to the full, unless there is reason to believe that judicial opinion is divided on the point in issue or, for some other reason, that there is an appreciable risk of a disagreement. In the last year there have been three or four appeals which have had to be re-argued. The use of two judge courts is therefore highly cost-effective in terms of the use of judicial manpower.

The next major consideration has been to try to reduce the time spent by the parties in court on the hearing of appeals. Such time is extremely expensive for them and it must not be wasted. As is, I think, well known, the solution has lain in enabling the members of the court to read at least the notice of appeal, the judgment under appeal and any skeleton arguments before the appeal is called on for hearing. The time spent in pre-reading is relatively small and the saving in court time is dramatic.

In the light of this very limited pre-reading, judges can, and if counsel shows any lack of enthusiasm for coming to the point, I personally do, open the appeal for him, summarising the background and identifying the point or points upon which we should be assisted by argument. At the other end of the hearing, we are again able to save time in court by handing down any judgments which have been reserved and put into writing. Reading out such judgments served only two purposes. It demonstrated that the Judges of the Court of Appeal could read, but the contrary has never seriously been contended. It also informed any member of the Press or public who chose to attend. The latter requirement, which is very important, is equally well achieved by giving copies of the judgment to the Press and allowing any member of the public who attends court when the judgments are handed down to read a copy. If and when an illiterate member of the public attends court and expresses an interest in the content of a judgment, we can always arranged for a member of the Civil Appeals Office to read it to him.

All this might be thought to enable the Court to hear far more appeals than was formerly the case, but this is not so. The "output" of the Court has risen only in proportion to the increased size of the Court and now runs at about 1100 appeals a year. Let me explain why this is so.

When I first joined the Court of Appeal, I was both impressed and oppressed by the never-ending supply of appeals and the difficulty in finding time to give proper thought to those which were especially difficult and the decision in which would provide an important precedent for the future. Although I am thought by some to be obsessed by the need to reduce, or at least contain, the number of appeals awaiting hearing, I am in truth equally concerned that members of the Court of Appeal should have all the time which they feel that they need to think round and about difficult decisions.

In fact the saving in time in court seems to be almost exactly balanced by the additional time spent out of court pre-reading and giving proper consideration to reasoned judgments. But this is a real gain in terms of expense to the parties and, although this is much more difficult to evaluate, should also be real gain in terms of the quality of our judgments.

This brings me to the true rôle of the Court of Appeal, as I see it. There are some who seem to regard it as the second round in a two round contest, where the second round is decisive. I profoundly disagree. As I see it, the Court of Appeal has two quite different functions. First, and possibly foremost, it is a court whose function is to develop and define the law where it has not previously been considered or is in doubt. In this respect it differs from the House of Lords in only two particulars. The Court of Appeal has far more material upon which to work. As I have said, it disposes of some 1100 appeals annually against the House of Lords output of about 70. In addition it is more confined by the doctrine of precedent than is the House of Lords. Its second rôle is to intervene in the exceptional case in which the trial judge has really fallen into error. My difficulty lies in persuading others that its second rôle is so limited.

To some extent this is a human problem. However much an appellate judge may, in theory, accept the idea that there may be no "right" decision, that the trial judge often has a discretion, that it is his exercise of discretion which should carry the day, and that the trial judge has seen and heard the witnesses, whilst we have only the transcripts, in practice other considerations obtrude, often quite unconsciously. Appellate judges are likely to be more experienced than trial judges, whom they will have known as counsel appearing before them. It may have been some time since they tried a case at first instance and they may have forgotten how much they then relied upon the "feel" which only the trial judge can have. They would be less than human if they did not suspect, rightly or wrongly,—since they are out of practice—that they could have tried the case better. I have no answer to this problem, save to air it and to express the view, not entirely in jest, that every Lord Justice should have on his desk, and read daily, a printed card bearing the legend "Do not forget, the trial judge just might have got it right".

One problem which will, I fancy, always face any Master of the Rolls is what to do about too many appeals chasing too few Lord Justices. This is not so much a matter of relieving pressure on the members of the court, as of ensuring that appellants who, in the event, will be successful in their appeals are not kept waiting with all the anxiety, loss and expense which is so often involved. The very fact that giving notice of appeal will delay the day of reckoning, may well prompt the institution of some appeals and the greater delay, the more there will be. We have already identified some areas where this is likely to be the case. The most obvious example is the tenant who has a possession order made against him and there are others. We give these appeals priority in order to discourage them. We also give priority to cases involving the custody or care and control of children, but this is for a quite different reason, namely, that a period of uncertainty can have far more serious effects upon a child that upon an adult.

But the real problem is to identify categories of appeal which have a low success rate and to create some screening process which will identify those appeals in that category which are truly arguable. If they are not arguable, they should not, in justice to those who have arguable appeals which are being delayed, be allowed to take up the time of the court. The first step is to acquire accurate and comprehensive statistical information by categories concerning success rates, the number of appeals involved and the maximum, minimum and average or medium period of time which elapses before they are disposed of. Given sufficient staff, this could be done manually, but the Civil Appeals Office is a relatively small unit. I therefore asked the Lord Chancellor to install a micro-computer system to monitor the work of the Court and this came into service on 1st October. It has already proved its worth in terms of listing. A gap suddenly appears in the list and it is necessary to identify suitable candidates to fill the gap from about 900 appeals awaiting hearing. The computer does this in a minute or two, when it would have taken hours without it. Teething troubles at present prevent it providing a broad spectrum of statistical information of the kind which is so badly needed, but these troubles will, I am quite sure, be overcome in the near future. The second step is to evolve an appropriate screening process, such as obtaining the leave of a Lord Justice, before the appeal can proceed. However, recent experience suggests that any such reform will prove controversial and it must clearly wait until we have the basic background information.

Finally I come to what I regard as my most important duty. This is to have an ever open door for those who are experiencing difficulty in the context of the work of the Court, whether they are members of the Court, other judges, practitioners or members of the public and to be a receptive listener to all who think that they can make a contribution to improving the service which the Civil Division of the Court of Appeal affords to the public. It was with a view to assuring you that the door is open and giving you some insight into my thinking, that I chose "The Problems of a Master of the Rolls" as the subject of this Address.

Further copies of this lecture may be obtained at £3 per copy from the Holdsworth Club, Faculty of Law, University of Birmingham, Edgbaston, Birmingham B15 2TT. If despatch by air mail is required the full cost of the postage should be added.